MARTIN LUTHER
KING JR.

MARTIN LUTHER KING JR.

ODYSSEYS

VALERIE BODDEN

CREATIVE EDUCATION · CREATIVE PAPERBACKS

Published by Creative Education and Creative Paperbacks
P.O. Box 227, Mankato, Minnesota 56002
Creative Education and Creative Paperbacks are imprints of
The Creative Company
www.thecreativecompany.us

Design by Blue Design (www.bluedes.com)
Production by Colin O'Dea
Art direction by Rita Marshall
Printed in the United States of America

Photographs by 123RF (Ruben Martinez Barricarte, Andrea
Izzotti), Alamy (Bettmann, Black Star, Everett Collection
Historical, Everett Collection Inc, MPVHistory, World History
Archive), Creative Commons Wikimedia (Associated Press,
Bellealert, John Vachon for U.S. Farm Security Administration/
Library of Congress, Warren K. Leffler/Library of Congress,
Warren K. Leffler/U.S. News & World Report/Library of
Congress, Yoichi Okamoto/LBJ Presidential Library, Yoichi
Okamoto/Lyndon Baines Johnson Library and Museum,
Johnny Silvercloud/Flickr, U.S. National Archives and Records
Administration), Getty Images (Bettmann, Michael Evans/
Hulton Archive, Hulton Archive/Stringer, Steve Schapiro/
Corbis, Stephen F. Somerstein), iStockphoto (Josie Desmarais,
TobinC)

Library of Congress Cataloging-in-Publication Data
Names: Bodden, Valerie, author.
Title: Martin Luther King Jr. / Valerie Bodden.
Series: Odysseys in peace.
Includes bibliographical references and index.
Summary: A biography of American civil rights leader Martin
Luther King Jr., examining his position as a voice of the
movement, as well as his emphasis on nonviolent resistance
and other social stances.
Identifiers: ISBN 978-1-64026-165-5 (hardcover) / ISBN
978-1-62832-728-1 (pbk) / ISBN 978-1-64000-283-8
(eBook)
This title has been submitted for CIP processing under LCCN
2019935255.

First Edition HC 9 8 7 6 5 4 3 2 1
First Edition PBK 9 8 7 6 5 4 3 2 1

CONTENTS

Introduction

His voice boomed over crowds, drawing them in with his rich baritone and swaying rhythms. From church pulpits, auditorium stages, and even the open air, Martin Luther King Jr. preached a message of nonviolence and racial unity to a nation rocked by racial tension. For many, King's message of nonviolent resistance made him a hero. To others, his disobedience of the law and desire to change the social order made him a

OPPOSITE: King's effective speaking style was notably marked by his use of repetition (with key phrases, such as "I have a dream") and cadence—changes in voice pitch, pace, and rhythm that give emphasis and add meaning to speech.

villain and a target to attack with hate.

Strongly influenced by both his Christian faith and the philosophy of nonviolence, King believed from a young age that he was meant to serve humanity. But he didn't know what form that service would take until he was thrust into a leadership position during a bus boycott in Montgomery, Alabama. Although at first hesitant to take the role, King eventually threw himself wholeheartedly into leadership of the civil rights movement.

Through marches, sit-ins, speeches, and more, King sought to stamp out racial injustice, poverty, and war. He faced insults, beatings, and jail time for his cause. When an assassin's bullet took his life at the age of 39, King was both one of the most beloved and one of the most hated men in America. Since his death, his legacy has grown. Today, he is recognized as one of the greatest leaders for peace the world has ever known.

Called to Lead

The man whose voice would one day move the world was born Michael King Jr. on January 15, 1929, in Atlanta, Georgia. When King was five, his father, Michael King Sr., changed both his own name and his son's from Michael to Martin Luther. He made the change after a trip to Germany, where Christian reformer Martin Luther had lived.

A leader of Atlanta's black community, Martin Luther King Sr. was

OPPOSITE: Inspired by the example of Jesus Christ and the techniques of Mahatma Gandhi, King formed his own philosophies regarding a nonviolent lifestyle, which he called a courageous way of life for its active resistance to evil.

pastor of Ebenezer Baptist Church. The King family lived in a comfortable house on Auburn Avenue, one of the wealthiest areas in the black part of Atlanta. King would later say that he never knew a moment of want during his childhood. More importantly, in King's view, his family always provided an example of love. King said his family's love made it "quite easy for me to lean more toward optimism than pessimism about human nature." Since his father, grandfather, uncle, and other family members were preachers, King was surrounded by religion as well, and he embraced it.

Despite his pleasant family life, King's early years were not without trouble. During King's childhood, life in the southern United States was strictly segregated, or divided by race. Laws dictated that blacks and whites could not use the same water fountains or restrooms, sit at the same lunch counters, or attend the same theaters. White children went to certain schools, while black children went to others. The law held that blacks and whites were to have "separate but equal" facilities. But facilities designated for African Americans were often in much poorer condition than those intended for whites.

Later in his life, King said that up until about the age of six, he was unaware of the deep racial divide in the South. His best friend was white, and the two of them played together nearly every day. But when it was time for them to start school, his white friend's father refused to let his son play with King anymore. When King asked his parents why, they had a frank discussion with him about race relations in the country. They made it clear to him that segregation was unnatural. They told him, "You are as good as anyone." Still, the experience planted hatred

Firsthand View of Discrimination

When he was 15, King won a speaking contest in Dublin, Georgia. His speech was titled "The Negro and the Constitution." In it, he said, "We cannot have an enlightened democracy with one great group living in ignorance. We cannot have a healthy nation with one-tenth of the people ill-nourished, sick, harboring germs of disease which recognize no color lines." Afterward, King and his teacher boarded a bus for the trip home. When a group of white passengers came on, the two black people were forced to give up their seats. They had to stand for the 90-mile (145 km) ride. This firsthand experience of discrimination fueled King's hatred of injustice.

King's father served as president of the Atlanta chapter of the National Association for the Advancement of Colored People (NAACP).

in the young boy for all whites. His parents reminded him that, as a Christian, he was to love everyone, even those who hated him. King remained unconvinced.

Although his parents told King to love whites, they also made it clear that they did not accept the system of segregation. King's father served as president of the Atlanta chapter of the National Association for the Advancement of Colored People (NAACP). He also actively resisted segregation. For example, when a clerk at a shoe store once asked Martin Sr. to move to the back of the store to be served, he refused and left the store.

Despite the racism he saw around him every day,

King was determined to succeed. According to biographer Godfrey Hodgson, King "remained convinced of the promise of America, and he was determined to share in that promise." King's perseverance saw him through school. Even though his grades weren't stellar, he finished high school at age 15, after skipping his senior year. By then, he knew he wanted to serve others. At first, he wanted to be a doctor or a lawyer, but he eventually decided to enter the ministry. As he later explained, "My call to the ministry ... was an inner urge calling me to serve humanity." For the next 10 years, King studied at Morehouse College in Atlanta, Crozer Seminary in Pennsylvania, and Boston University. In college, King developed his distinct speaking style as well as a growing interest in racial justice. He began to rethink his hatred for whites as he encountered white teachers and classmates who were active in the civil rights struggle.

While in college, King also was exposed to the non-violent philosophy of Indian activist Mahatma Gandhi. Gandhi promoted the concept of satyagraha, or "truth force," to bring about social change. Gandhi's nonviolent political resistance involved taking direct, nonviolent action through marches, boycotts, and other forms of peaceful noncooperation. As King studied Gandhi's teachings, he came to believe that working for peace did not mean allowing evil to happen. Instead, it meant actively resisting evil with love.

While in Boston, King met Coretta Scott. The two married in 1953 and eventually had four children together. The next year, the newlyweds moved to Montgomery, Alabama, where King began to serve as pastor of Dexter Avenue Baptist Church. Almost as soon as he arrived in

Life in the North

The summer before he entered Morehouse College, King worked on a farm in Connecticut. He wrote to his father about his amazement at what he found there. "There [is] no discrimination at all and the white people here are very nice," he wrote. "We go to any place we want and sit anywhere we want to." Although he appreciated the relative equality blacks enjoyed in the North, King also noted subtle forms of discrimination. After later moving to Boston, for example, he found that apartments that were supposedly for rent had "suddenly ... just been rented" when the owners learned he was black.

Montgomery, King joined local civil rights organizations, including the NAACP and the Alabama Council on Human Relations.

King had been in Montgomery only about a year when leadership of the community's civil rights movement fell directly into his lap. On December 1, 1955, Rosa Parks, a local seamstress and civil rights worker, was arrested for refusing to give up her seat on a city bus for a white man. Afterward, a group of the city's black ministers agreed to arrange a boycott of the city's bus system. They created an organization known as the Montgomery Improvement Association (MIA) and nominated King to lead it. King later said that if he'd had time to think about the nomination, he probably would have declined it. Instead, he found himself at the helm of what would become a nearly year-long battle to end

On December 1, 1955, Rosa Parks, a local seamstress and civil rights worker, was arrested for refusing to give up her seat on a city bus for a white man.

segregation on city buses in Montgomery.

In his new leadership position, King spoke to thousands at mass meetings, reminding them why they were fighting to end segregation. "We are determined here in Montgomery to work and fight until justice runs down like water and righteousness like a mighty stream," he told them, using images and phrases from the Bible, as he would continue to do in his speeches throughout his life. During the course of the protest, King was arrested and jailed for the first time. He and many other participants faced threats and violence. On one occasion, King's home was firebombed, but no one was hurt.

The constant stress eventually took a toll, and King found himself in his kitchen late one night, praying: "I am here taking a stand for what I believe is right. But Lord, I must confess that I'm weak now, I'm faltering. I'm losing my courage." King later said that after his prayer, he was overcome with a sense of peace, and his fear disappeared. He believed God was telling him to continue standing up for justice and truth.

On November 13, 1956, the U.S. Supreme Court affirmed that Alabama and Montgomery's bus segregation was unconstitutional. The state and city were ordered to desegregate their buses. The decision was a relief to King. But his work was just beginning.

"Nonviolence is a powerful and just weapon. Indeed, it is a weapon unique in history, which cuts without wounding.... It is a sword that heals."

- Martin Luther King Jr., *Why We Can't Wait*, 1963

Voice of a People

King and the other leaders of the Montgomery bus boycott were determined to build on their success. They wanted to expand their movement across the entire South. In January 1957, 60 black ministers formed the Southern Christian Leadership Conference (SCLC), headquartered in Atlanta. King was chosen as the organization's president. The SCLC's goal was to work toward desegregation and black rights.

OPPOSITE: In the years following the SCLC's founding, integrated marches for civil rights became somewhat standard, owing to the movement's emphasis on nonviolent tactics for protesting segregation.

27

In addition to heading the SCLC, King also served as co-pastor at Ebenezer after he moved to Atlanta with his family in 1960.

King's leadership in Montgomery had brought him worldwide attention. Now he used that attention as he traveled the country to drum up support for the SCLC. Everywhere, crowds thronged to hear him. His activities were often covered on national television, making him instantly recognizable. In his speeches, King repeatedly emphasized his desire to see a day "when all God's children, black men and white men, Jews and Gentiles, Protestants and Catholics, will be able to join hands." He wanted all people to form a "beloved community" in which prejudice would be replaced by love.

One of King's most famous campaigns took him to Birmingham, Alabama, which had a reputation as one of the most segregated cities in the South. His goal when he arrived there in April 1963 was to end segregation in the city's downtown businesses. Early in the campaign, King was arrested for violating a court order against marching. He spent his first 24 hours behind bars in solitary confinement. He later wrote that those hours were "the longest, the most frightening and bewildering ... I have lived."

While he was in jail, a group of white ministers published a letter to King in the local newspaper. In it,

Not Guilty

In February 1960, King was arrested on felony charges of tax evasion and perjury. Although King had previously gone to jail willingly for disobeying laws he saw as unjust, the arrest this time was a political move intended to stall the civil rights movement. On May 28, King stood trial before an all-white jury. They returned a verdict of not guilty. King said his **acquittal** proved there were good white people in the South. Still, the judge in the case expressed his amazement that a white jury had acquitted a black man, calling the verdict the "most surprising thing" he had seen in his career.

they referred to him as an outsider who had come into their city to lead ill-timed protests. After reading the article, King wrote a lengthy response. His letter has since become one of his most famous explanations for why the civil rights movement had to happen when and how it did. The purpose of his nonviolent campaigns, he wrote, was to create enough tension that those in power would be moved to negotiate. As to why the campaign had to happen now, King wrote, "For years now I have heard the word 'Wait!'... This 'Wait' has almost always meant 'Never.'"

By the time King was released from jail nine days later, the Birmingham campaign was in danger of fizzling out. At the suggestion of his adviser James Bevel, King reluctantly agreed to involve students in the protest. On May 2, hundreds of children, ranging in age from 6 to 16, turned out to march. By the next day, more than 1,000 were in jail. Birmingham police brought out the police dogs and high-powered fire hoses to deal with the masses of student protesters. Media coverage captured images of dogs lunging at child protesters and police beating women with clubs. The nation was horrified. People everywhere raised an outcry. Many who had formerly ignored or opposed the civil rights movement now offered it their support. In the face of public scrutiny, Birmingham's leaders agreed to work toward desegregation. King's recognition and status quickly rose. To many, he was the voice of an oppressed people.

King continued to use that voice in campaigns across the South. But many Americans of the time—and still today—agreed that his crowning achievement was the March on Washington for Jobs and Freedom. On August

28, 1963, before 200,000-some people gathered in front of the Lincoln Memorial in Washington, D.C., King delivered his now-famous "I Have a Dream" speech. He told the electrified crowd, "I have a dream that one day this nation will rise up and live out the true meaning of its creed—we hold these truths to be self-evident that all men are created equal." As the people clapped and cried out, King continued, "I have a dream that my four little children will one day live in a nation where they will not be judged by the color of their skin but by the content of their character."

By 1964, the nonviolent approach had started to produce national results. On July 2, president Lyndon B. Johnson signed the Civil Rights Act of 1964, which outlawed segregation and discrimination. Later that year, King's contributions to peace and justice were honored

In 1963, Hoover began wiretapping King's phones and hotel rooms. He found no sign that King supported communism.

when he was presented with the Nobel Peace Prize.

But not everyone held King up as a hero. For years, J. Edgar Hoover, director of the Federal Bureau of Investigation (FBI), had been convinced King was a communist. In 1963, Hoover began wiretapping King's phones and hotel rooms. He found no sign that King supported communism. Instead, he found purported evidence of extramarital affairs. Hoover threatened to use that information to discredit King's movement.

In addition, King faced growing criticism from younger activists, who had come to see his nonviolent tactics as weak. Black nationalist leader Malcolm X called King's

The 1963 March on Washington coincided with the hundredth anniversary of the Emancipation Proclamation and was organized by activist Bayard Rustin and his cadre of volunteers.

Black nationalist leader Malcolm X called King's tactics "criminal" because he taught "a man not to defend himself when he is the constant victim of brutal attacks."

tactics "criminal" because he taught "a man not to defend himself when he is the constant victim of brutal attacks." Others outside the civil rights movement believed just the opposite. They accused King of traveling into peaceful cities and causing trouble by provoking law enforcement with marches and other nonviolent activities. Even those who supported King sometimes accused him of coming into a community, stirring things up, and then leaving without waiting for any real changes to occur.

Despite such criticisms, King pushed on. Now that segregation had been made illegal, he turned to voter registration. In many Southern cities, blacks were kept from registering to vote through threats and violence. In other places, they had to complete difficult literacy tests. In early 1965, civil rights groups focused their attention on a voter registration drive in Selma, Alabama. On March 7, a group of demonstrators set out for a march from Selma to Montgomery. But as the marchers crested the steep Edmund Pettus Bridge over the Alabama River, they were met by armed patrolmen wearing gas masks. The officers unleashed tear gas on the protesters, beat them with clubs wrapped in barbed wire, and jabbed them with electric cattle prods.

Days later, King tried to lead another march. This time, when told to turn back, the demonstrators first knelt to pray. Then, led by King, they turned around. On March 21, with permission to march finally granted,

OPPOSITE President Johnson signed several landmark laws, including the Civil Rights Act of 1964 and the Voting Rights Act of 1965, plus those related to Medicare, children's health, clean air, housing, and more.

demonstrators set out for Montgomery. With military protection, they crossed the bridge without incident. Four days later, 25,000 marchers arrived in Montgomery, where King told them the fight for their rights was almost won.

He was correct. On August 6, 1965, Johnson signed the Voting Rights Act of 1965. The act prohibited discrimination in voter registration. With that battle won, King turned to his next challenge.

"We will meet the forces of hate with the power of love.... We will match your capacity to inflict suffering with our capacity to endure suffering.... Bomb our homes and we will still love you.... We will so appeal to your heart and conscience that we will win you in the process."

- Martin Luther King Jr., during the Birmingham campaign

To the End

For 10 years, King had been fighting segregation and discrimination in the American South. But he knew conditions in many northern cities weren't much better, even if discrimination took more subtle forms. There, blacks lived in rundown ghettos plagued by drugs, unemployment, and poverty. Many black neighborhoods had inadequate access to healthcare and schools. King came to believe that the greatest injustice of all was

OPPOSITE: In cities across the country, decades of discriminatory policies determined where people of color lived; where people live affects all other aspects of life, from access to food and jobs to safety and quality of education.

43

poverty, and he committed to an all-out, nonviolent war against it.

One of the worst northern cities in terms of African American living conditions was Chicago. King decided to make his next campaign there. In January 1966, he moved his family from their modest home in Atlanta to a tiny apartment on the west side of Chicago. From there, King led marches through Chicago's white neighborhoods. Residents of those neighborhoods responded by jeering, launching bottles and bricks, and burning marchers' parked cars. Twice during the summer of 1966, riots broke out. By the end of the summer, Chicago's mayor Richard Daley had agreed to end discrimination in housing practices. But many saw the mayor's agreement as a false victory, since it did not include any enforcement measures.

As events turned violent in Chicago, so did civil rights workers continue to face violence elsewhere. In June 1966, King and other activists poured into Mississippi after civil rights leader James Meredith was shot during a voting rights march there. The leaders of SCLC and other civil rights groups agreed to hold a joint march in response. Although King continued to insist on nonviolence, others had grown impatient with this technique. On June 16, Stokely Carmichael, leader of the Student Nonviolent Coordinating Committee (SNCC), told the marchers, "What we need is black power." His followers quickly took up the cry.

King tried to reason with those advocating the use of force. "We are 10 percent of the population of this nation," he said, "I would be misleading you if I made you feel that we could win a violent campaign.... The minute we start, we will end up getting many people killed unnecessarily." King said he refused to stoop to the level of those who were oppressing them. The news media was quick to pick up on the rift in the movement.

Learning from Failure

Although King is best known for his successful campaigns such as in Birmingham and Selma, he also suffered a number of failures. Among the worst was a campaign to desegregate Albany, Georgia, in 1961. Over the course of the campaign, King was jailed three times. Even so, he failed to win any concessions from the city's government. He later said the reason for his failure in Albany was his attempt to integrate everything in the city at once. He learned his lesson and from then on targeted specific aspects of a city's segregation—such as at lunch counters or stores—for his campaigns.

Some speculated that King's position as leader of the civil rights movement had come to an end.

But King's reputation was in for an even greater blow. Since the early 1960s, the U.S. had been aiding South Vietnam in its war against communist North Vietnam. Beginning in 1965, President Johnson escalated U.S. involvement by sending hundreds of thousands of soldiers to Vietnam. King, who had always hated war, disagreed with Johnson's decision. But he at first worried that speaking out against the war would endanger the civil rights movement. By 1967, his conscience would no longer allow him to remain silent. On April 4, 1967, at Riverside Church in New York, King told listeners that he could not support a war that was "taking the black young men who had been crippled by our society and sending them eight thousand miles away to guarantee

Beginning in 1965, President Johnson escalated U.S. involvement by sending hundreds of thousands of soldiers to Vietnam.

liberties in Southeast Asia which they had not found in southwest Georgia or East Harlem." King's speech was met with open hostility by most newspapers in the country. Critics said King should stick to civil rights. To King, however, justice and peace were linked, and he continued to speak out against the war despite the unpopularity of his stance.

King soon started on another unpopular project, which he called the Poor People's Campaign. His goal was to bring poor people of all races and from all parts of the country to Washington, D.C. There they would hold marches, demonstrations, and even a camp-in. They

ORIGINAL
ACCO ROAD
LES GRAPEWIN
is This FREEDOM?
EMOCRACY i ou AIM
DEMOCRACY is our AIM
Equality is all we WANT!
This EDOM?

would refuse to leave until lawmakers took steps to end poverty. King traveled the country, trying to drum up support for the Poor People's Campaign. But he met with little enthusiasm from either the wealthy supporters he would need to fund the movement or the poor people who were supposed to carry out the campaign.

By early 1968, the strain of the campaign was taking a toll on King, who had fallen into a severe depression. He admitted that at times he felt worn and exhausted, and he began to speak more often about the inevitability of his own death. He had long since grown used to the idea that he could be killed at any time and had gotten over his fear of death. But that didn't mean the constant work and daily threats didn't get to him. "I'm frankly tired of marching," he said in 1968. "I'm tired of going to jail. Living every day under the threat of death, I feel

Behind Bars

Although jail cells became familiar sites to King, he never got used to the feeling of being in jail. On one occasion, he wrote: "Jail is depressing because it shuts off the world. It leaves one caught in the dull monotony of sameness. It is almost like being dead while one still lives." Ever the optimist, King found a bright side, even to his time behind bars. "The only way that I adjust to it is to constantly remind myself that this self-imposed suffering is for a great cause and purpose. This realization takes a little of the agony and a little of the depression away."

"Maybe we just have to give up and let violence take its course," he told his associates. But King shook off his despair and returned to Memphis on April 3, 1968.

discouraged every now and then and feel my work's in vain, but then the Holy Spirit revives my soul again."

King pressed on. In the spring of 1968, he was asked to travel to Memphis, Tennessee, to support striking sanitation workers. From the beginning of the march on March 28, King could tell something was "just wrong." About halfway through, a group of young activists belonging to a militant Black Power group pulled the wooden sticks off their signs and used them to smash store windows. Some looted the stores, while others threw bottles, stones, and bricks. King's aides rushed him off the scene—to protect both his life and his reputation as a nonviolent leader. As King watched the television coverage, he despaired. "Maybe we just have to give up and let violence take its course," he told his associates.

But King shook off his despair and returned to Memphis on April 3, 1968. That night, in the midst of a raging thunderstorm, he spoke to a crowd of more than 2,000 at Mason Temple. His comments punctuated by thunder, wind, and the shouts and claps of his listeners, King turned reflective. "Like anybody, I would like to live a long life.... But I'm not concerned about that now. I just want to do God's will. And He's allowed me to go up to the mountain. And I've looked over. And I've seen the Promised Land. I may not get there with you. But I want you to know tonight, that we, as a people, will get to the Promised Land!"

King spent most of the next day at the Lorraine Motel with his aides. That night, as he was preparing for dinner, he stepped onto the balcony outside his second-story room. Just as he leaned over the railing to speak to his aides in the parking lot below, a gunshot ripped through the still night. King fell to the balcony floor. At 39, the world's most famous civil rights leader was dead.

QUOTE

"We've got to give ourselves to this struggle until the end. Nothing could be more tragic than to stop at this point.... We've got to see it through.... Be concerned about your brother.... Either we go up together or we go down together."

- Martin Luther King Jr., April 3, 1968, speech at Mason Temple

Lasting Legacy

Only hours after King was pronounced dead, President Johnson went on television to announce the news to a stunned nation. As he reported King's death, Johnson also urged the nation to remain calm. "I ask every citizen to reject the blind violence that has struck Dr. King," he said. "We can achieve nothing by lawlessness."

Despite Johnson's plea, riots soon broke out in more than 100 U.S. cities. Many African Americans reported

OPPOSITE: In response to the systemic violence against black people that persists in modern times, movements such as Black Lives Matter "intervene in violence inflicted against black communities."

feeling as if a member of their own family had been killed. According to author and professor Michael Eric Dyson, "Black America mourned King's murder so deeply because it felt like *our* murder. King's death felt like the death of black progress, the death of black justice, the death of black hope, because its most passionate voice had been sniped into silence."

Only days after King's death, the march he had been planning in Memphis was held as a tribute to him. On April 8, more than 20,000 people gathered in the city. Led by Coretta and the couple's three oldest children, the marchers walked silently through the streets. Afterward, Coretta addressed the crowd. "How many men must die before we can really have a free and true and peaceful society?" she asked. "If we can catch the spirit, and the true meaning of this experience, I believe that this nation can be transformed into a society of love, of justice, peace, and brotherhood."

The next day, thousands of people flooded Atlanta for King's funeral. Millions more watched on television. The day began with a service for family and friends at Ebenezer Baptist Church. They listened to a recording of one of King's last sermons at Ebenezer, in which he talked about how he'd like to be remembered after his death. "I'd like somebody to mention that Martin Luther King Jr. tried to give his life serving others," he said. After the service, more than 150,000 people marched four miles (6.4 km) behind a mule-drawn wagon pulling King's casket. It was, Coretta later wrote, King's "last great march." The march ended at Morehouse College, where King's former mentor, Benjamin Mays, delivered his eulogy.

To Catch a Killer

It took two months, but King's killer was finally identified as James Earl Ray, an escaped convict, and captured. On March 10, 1969, Ray pleaded guilty to King's murder, though he never offered a motive for it. He was sentenced to 99 years in prison. Three days later, however, Ray recanted his plea. Until his death in prison in 1998, he insisted on his innocence. His change of heart led many to believe Ray may have been hired to kill King. Theories about who may have hired him ranged from the Ku Klux Klan to black militants to the FBI. However, no evidence has ever indicated Ray worked for anyone but himself.

OPPOSITE Peaceful demonstrators carried on King's legacy in the months immediately following his death, marching for fairer wages and other measures of economic justice.

Despite their grief, King's coworkers in the civil rights movement were determined to carry on his life's work. Only a month after King's death, more than 2,000 demonstrators began to arrive in Washington, D.C., for the Poor People's Campaign. As King had hoped, there were people from all races and nationalities, all united by their poverty. The demonstrators sheltered in crudely constructed huts of plywood. They demanded a minimum yearly income for all Americans, an end to hunger, and a plan to fix the nation's ghettos. But within a week, the campaign began to fall apart. By late June, the group's permit had expired. They were forced to disband without any of their demands met. To many, this defeat was further proof of how indispensable King's leadership had been.

King's death left a gaping hole in the nonviolent

Only days after King's death, President Johnson signed the Civil Rights Act of 1968.

civil rights movement as well. Only days after King's death, President Johnson signed the Civil Rights Act of 1968, which included the Fair Housing Act. This provision—which King had been pushing for before his death—outlawed discrimination in housing. Many lawmakers saw the act as a way to honor King. Its passage proved to be the last great victory of the nonviolent civil rights movement.

Although King's colleagues continued to advocate nonviolence, their message seemed irrelevant to most black Americans. As they saw it, King's death proved that nonviolence had failed. "King was the last prince of nonviolence [and] nonviolence is now a dead philosophy," declared Floyd McKissick of the Congress of Racial Equality (CORE). More and more blacks came to favor the militant tactics advocated by groups such as CORE and the Black Panthers. According to young activist Hazel Mack, the Black Panthers were appealing because "they said if you die, at least die fighting back."

Over the years, as African Americans made inroads in areas of society that had once been closed to them, mass protests largely came to an end. By the 1980s and 1990s, many of the changes King had fought so hard for seemed to have been realized. Schools, stores, and other institutions were fully integrated. African Americans not only voted but held elected positions. In 2008, Barack Obama was elected as the country's first African Amer-

Modest Lifestyle

Although King could have been among the wealthiest black men in Atlanta, he insisted on maintaining a modest lifestyle. He drew only a small salary from Ebenezer Baptist Church and refused to accept payment from the SCLC. He earned more than $200,000 a year from speaking engagements, but he funneled most of that money into the civil rights movement. Money earned from the books he wrote went to Morehouse College. Even the $50,000 he received for his Nobel Prize went to SCLC charities. Until the mid-1960s, King even refused to purchase a house. He didn't want to set himself apart from the people whose cause he championed.

ican president, leading many Americans to hope King's vision for a united America had finally become reality.

But life for many African Americans remained difficult. By the early 21st century, black men made up half of the nation's prison population. Many African Americans continued to live in the types of ghettos King had deplored. In 2013, police killings of unarmed black men sparked the Black Lives Matter movement. Activists in this movement used many of King's nonviolent techniques, including sit-ins, protests, and marches. In 2018, on the 50th anniversary of King's death, the civil rights leader's son Martin Luther King III declared the Black Lives Matter movement was a continuation of his father's legacy.

Today, people in the U.S. and more than 100 other countries annually honor that legacy on Martin Luther

King Day. Memorials around the U.S. are also dedicated to the slain leader. The Lorraine Motel, where King was assassinated, has become a landmark and now houses the National Civil Rights Museum. The Martin Luther King Jr. Memorial in Washington, D.C., is a short walk from the Lincoln Memorial, where King delivered his famous "I Have a Dream" speech. Millions travel to Atlanta every year to visit King's grave. But the grave isn't only a shrine to a fallen leader. It is surrounded by the King Center, a nonprofit social justice organization founded by Coretta Scott King. Led today by the couple's daughter Bernice King, the center is dedicated to "inspiring new generations to carry forward his unfinished work."

Although King's work continues, some people worry that in the years since his death, his image has been softened. While King is widely admired today, it is easy

Loved by All

Although King's goal was to create a beloved community, he was nowhere near loved by all at the time of his death. In 1966, 63 percent of Americans overall—and 72 percent of whites—had an unfavorable view of King. After his death, however, King's approval ratings soared. By the late 1980s, the majority of Americans had a favorable opinion of him. And by 2011, a full 94 percent of Americans viewed King in a positive light. But only about half felt his dream of racial equality had been realized.

to forget that during his lifetime, he was hated as much as he was loved. He preached equal rights for people of all races and condemned war and poverty. His message jolted the nation, and he was jailed, beaten, threatened, and ultimately killed for it. Today, however, according to biographer Godfrey Hodgson, King is often viewed as an "unthreatening, relatively conservative leader, when in reality his vision was profoundly and unrelentingly radical." Such radical work has led him to be recognized as one of the world's greatest nonviolent advocates—one whose goal was to spread peace to all people. Most of all, today he is remembered as a man who had a dream—for his children, for his country, and for the world.

"I don't think the important thing really is how long you live, but how well you live. And I'm not concerned about my longevity or the quantity of my life, but the quality of my life."

- Martin Luther King Jr., interview, December 1967

Timeline

1929 The future civil rights leader is born Michael King Jr. on January 15, in Atlanta, Georgia.

1953 On June 18, King marries Coretta Scott, and the two eventually have four children together.

1954 King moves to Montgomery, Alabama, to serve as pastor of Dexter Avenue Baptist Church.

1955 King is elected president of the Montgomery Improvement Association and begins leadership of a yearlong bus boycott to end segregation.

1957 The Southern Christian Leadership Conference is founded in January, with King as president.

1963 In April, King is arrested in Birmingham, Alabama, and writes "Letter from a Birmingham Jail," outlining the reasons for the civil rights movement.

1964 President Lyndon B. Johnson signs the Civil Rights Act of 1964 on July 2, which outlaws segregation and discrimination.

1964 King receives the Nobel Peace Prize on July 2.

1965 On March 21, King leads a march from Selma to Montgomery, Alabama, telling marchers their victory is coming soon.

1965 President Johnson signs the Voting Rights Act on August 6, prohibiting discrimination in voter registration.

1966   In January, King moves his family to Chicago, where
he starts a campaign for equal-opportunity housing,
sparking riots.

1967   King speaks out publicly against the Vietnam War for
the first time in April.

1968   On April 4, King is assassinated in Memphis, Tennessee.

1968   A silent march is held in Memphis in King's honor on
April 8; his funeral in Atlanta the next day is attended by
more than 150,000 people.

1968   On April 11, President Johnson signs the Civil Rights Act
of 1968, which includes the Fair Housing Act, outlawing
discrimination in housing.

2013   The Black Lives Matter movement, sparked by police
killings of unarmed black men, adopts many of King's
nonviolent tactics.

Selected Bibliography

Carson, Clayborne, ed. *The Autobiography of Martin Luther
King, Jr.* New York: Grand Central, 1998.

Chappell, David L. *Waking from the Dream: The Struggle for
Civil Rights in the Shadow of Martin Luther King, Jr.* New
York: Random House, 2014.

Dyson, Michael Eric. *April 4, 1968: Martin Luther King, Jr.'s
Death and How It Changed America.* New York: Perseus,
2008.

Frady, Marshall. *Martin Luther King, Jr.* New York: Penguin,
2002.

Hodgson, Godfrey. *Martin Luther King.* Ann Arbor: University of Michigan, 2009.

Posner, Gerald. *Killing the Dream: James Earl Ray and the Assassination of Martin Luther King, Jr.* New York: Random House, 1998.

Sides, Hampton. *Hellhound on His Trail: The Electrifying Account of the Largest Manhunt in American History.* New York: Anchor Books, 2011.

Sokol, Jason. *The Heavens Might Crack: The Death and Legacy of Martin Luther King Jr.* New York: Basic Books, 2018.

Endnotes

acquittal	judgment that a person is not guilty of a crime
Black Panthers	organization founded in 1966 that advocated active self-defense against police brutality, the arming of all African Americans, and the release of all African Americans from jail
boycott	a form of protest involving refusal to purchase or use certain goods or a withdrawal from commercial or social relationships
communist	a supporter of the political theory of communism, which promotes public ownership of all property and industry

CORE	civil rights organization founded in 1942 to work against segregation and discrimination, best known for leading Freedom Rides—integrated bus rides through Southern states that tested desegregation laws (Congress of Racial Equality)
literacy tests	tests of a person's ability to read and write that many Southern states required African Americans to take before registering to vote
Mahatma Gandhi	Indian politician and activist who led nonviolent protests against British rule of his country in the early 1900s
Malcolm X	African American leader who promoted racial pride and black power and criticized King's nonviolent approach to gaining civil rights
NAACP	interracial organization founded in 1909 to work toward ending segregation and ensuring equal rights for African Americans (National Association for the Advancement of Colored People)
sit-ins	nonviolent protests in which demonstrators sit in a specific location and refuse to leave; during the civil rights movement, many sit-ins were held at segregated lunch counters

SNCC	civil rights organization founded in 1960 to organize student sit-ins at lunch counters; at first nonviolent, by the late 1960s, SNCC had adopted a more militant approach (Student Nonviolent Coordinating Committee)
wiretapping	using hidden electronic recording devices to secretly listen to a person's telephone calls

Websites

The King Center
http://www.thekingcenter.org/

Learn more about King's life and legacy and how the King Center continues to carry out his mission.

National Civil Rights Museum at the Lorraine Motel
https://www.civilrightsmuseum.org/

Track the struggle for racial equality from its earliest days through King's life and work and beyond.

Index